BEAUTIFUL BOWLS
and
COLOURFUL CREATURES

by Kath Danswan

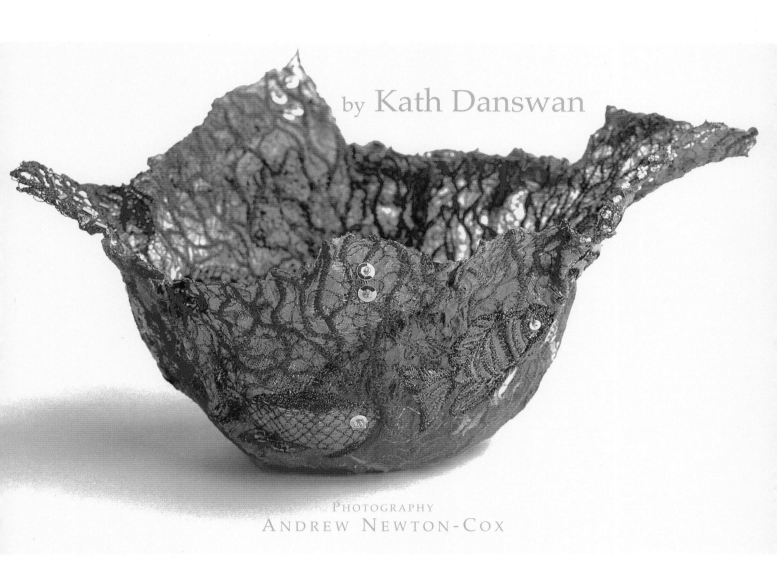

PHOTOGRAPHY
ANDREW NEWTON-COX

THE LINEN PRESS

I would like to dedicate this first book to my mother Phyllis Owens who instilled the love of embroidery in me from an early age, and my husband Geoff who has encouraged me to continue with it.

Kathleen

First Published in Great Britain in 2006 by
THE LINEN PRESS
PO BOX 3143
Marlborough
Wiltshire
SN8 1WB

www. linenpress.org.uk

The author has made every effort to ensure that all instructions in this book are safe and accurate and cannot accept liability for any resulting damage loss or injury to either person or property whether direct or consequential howsoever arising.

The author of this book has asserted her moral rights.

ISBN-13: 978-0-9554394-0-7
ISBN-10:   0-9554394-0-X

A CIP record for this book is available from The British Library

Designed and Produced by
THE LINEN PRESS
PO Box 3143
Marlborough
Wiltshire
SN8 1WB

www.linenpress.org.uk

Editor: Deena Beverley
Designer: Angel Hughes
Photographer: Andrew Newton-Cox
Additional Text: Deena Beverley

Printed in England

9 8 7 6 5 4 3 2

Contents

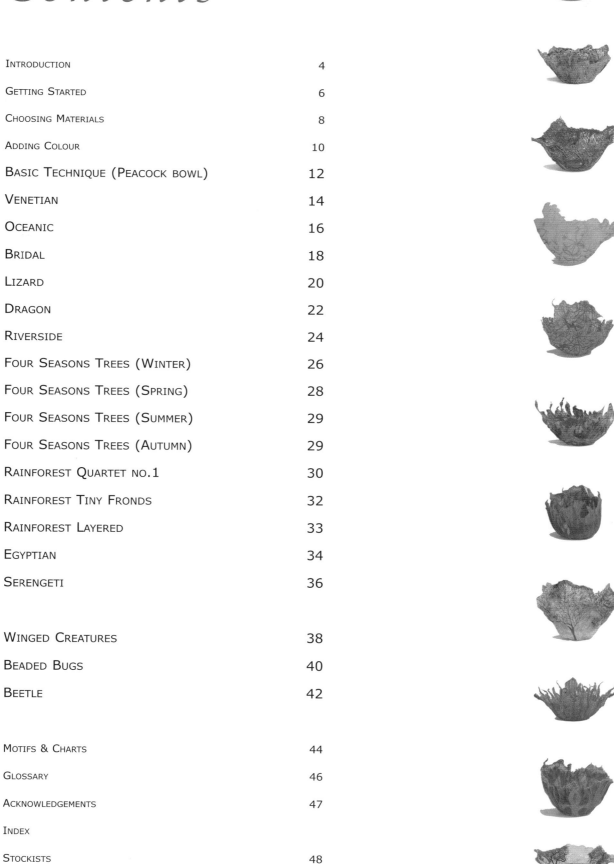

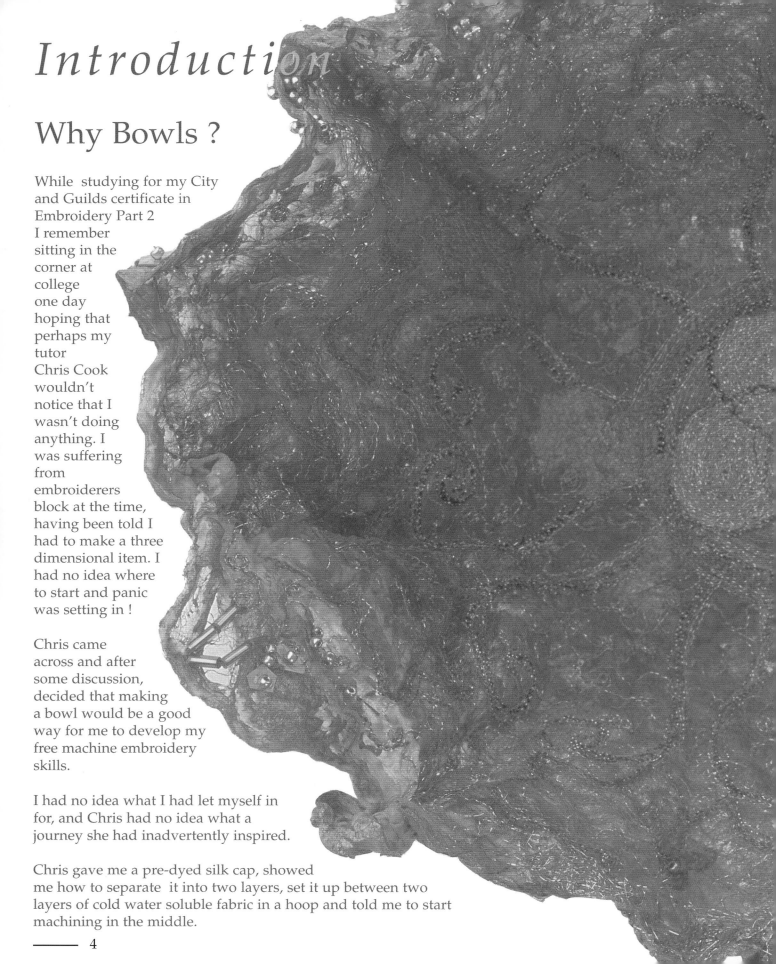

Introduction

Why Bowls ?

While studying for my City and Guilds certificate in Embroidery Part 2 I remember sitting in the corner at college one day hoping that perhaps my tutor Chris Cook wouldn't notice that I wasn't doing anything. I was suffering from embroiderers block at the time, having been told I had to make a three dimensional item. I had no idea where to start and panic was setting in !

Chris came across and after some discussion, decided that making a bowl would be a good way for me to develop my free machine embroidery skills.

I had no idea what I had let myself in for, and Chris had no idea what a journey she had inadvertently inspired.

Chris gave me a pre-dyed silk cap, showed me how to separate it into two layers, set it up between two layers of cold water soluble fabric in a hoop and told me to start machining in the middle.

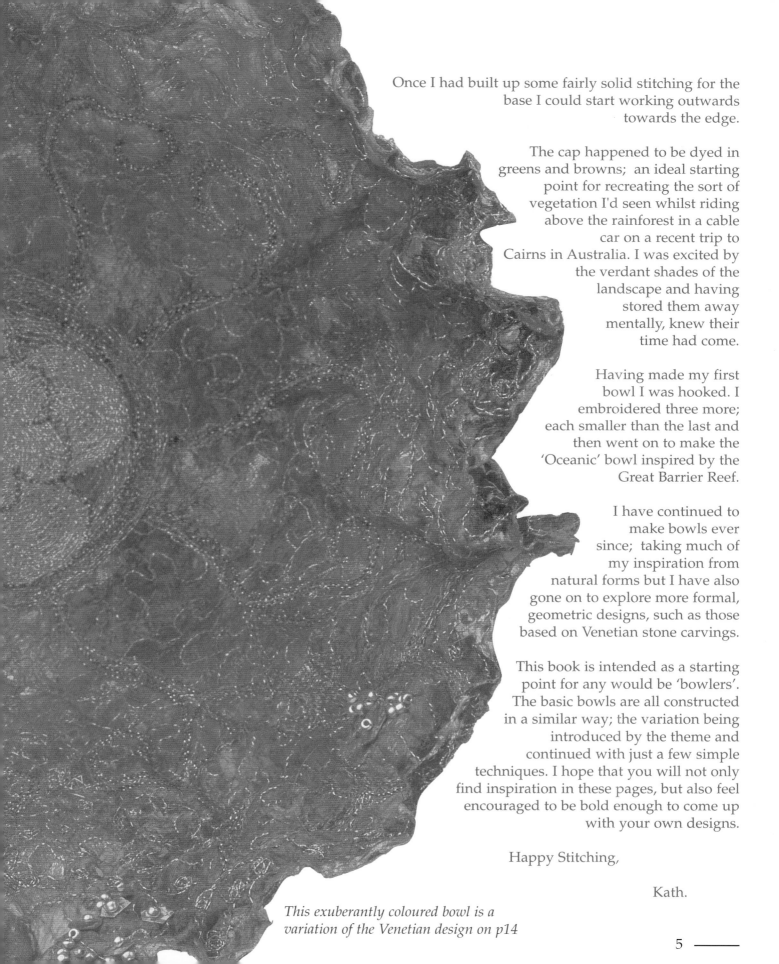

Once I had built up some fairly solid stitching for the base I could start working outwards towards the edge.

The cap happened to be dyed in greens and browns; an ideal starting point for recreating the sort of vegetation I'd seen whilst riding above the rainforest in a cable car on a recent trip to Cairns in Australia. I was excited by the verdant shades of the landscape and having stored them away mentally, knew their time had come.

Having made my first bowl I was hooked. I embroidered three more; each smaller than the last and then went on to make the 'Oceanic' bowl inspired by the Great Barrier Reef.

I have continued to make bowls ever since; taking much of my inspiration from natural forms but I have also gone on to explore more formal, geometric designs, such as those based on Venetian stone carvings.

This book is intended as a starting point for any would be 'bowlers'. The basic bowls are all constructed in a similar way; the variation being introduced by the theme and continued with just a few simple techniques. I hope that you will not only find inspiration in these pages, but also feel encouraged to be bold enough to come up with your own designs.

Happy Stitching,

Kath.

This exuberantly coloured bowl is a variation of the Venetian design on p14

Getting Started

The beauty of all the projects in this book is that they do not require any special equipment. The average embroiderer will have most of it already and any additional requirements can be bought relatively cheaply. Just taking a little care over choices at this stage can make all the difference to the finished article and your enjoyment in its making.

Sewing Machine

You do not have to have an all singing, all dancing model for the projects in this book. You need a machine which has straight and zigzag stitch. You also need to be able to disengage the feed dogs for free machining, either by lowering them, or by fitting a darning plate over them. I have used a basic Bernina throughout, which has a feed dog lowering facility, and also the very useful feature of being able to adjust the width of zigzag stitch manually during stitching.

Sewing Machine Needles

You will need to have a good stock of machine needles as they become blunt very quickly.

I generally use a Metallic 80/12 when stitching with a metallic thread and Embroidery 90/14 or 100/16 when using an ordinary thread.

If the metallic thread starts to shred then it could be time to change the needle as the thread can wear the 'eye'.

Sewing Machine Tools

Because you are working your machine for long stretches at a time you will need to oil it regularly with sewing machine oil, applied according to the manufacturer's directions. Some machines do not need oiling.

A small paintbrush is useful to brush away any lint that collects around the bobbin casing.

Sewing Machine Accessories

Your machine will need a darning or embroidery foot. There are several types, but I prefer the spring loaded, front opening foot as it is easier to see where you are stitching. However if your machine does not have such a foot, then use a darning foot with a large hole.

Transfer and Marking Equipment

The Lizard and Serengeti bowls feature motifs transferred onto Solusheet water soluble fabric and directly applied to the silk cap. The motifs can be traced straight onto the Solusheet using an HB pencil or a fine tipped waterproof pen. Using a waterproof pen is essential so that the ink will not wash into the fabric when the water soluble fabric is washed away.

HAND SEWING EQUIPMENT
Needles and Threads
For the projects in this book you will need a beading needle and a fine sharp needle for adding sequins, small beads and details such as cobwebs. Match threads to background colours when adding beads.

Pins
If you need to pin motifs or additional fabrics in place during stitching, I recommend using glass headed pins as these are easier to see, and therefore avoid with the foot when you are machining.

Scissors and cutting tools
You will need a pair of shears for cutting the water soluble fabric and a pair of small embroidery scissors for snipping off threads close to the work. Wire cutters will be useful for beading work. A fine tipped soldering iron is invaluable for simultaneously trimming and sealing organza edges eg. dragonfly wings.

Embroidery Hoop
You will need a spring clip embroidery hoop with a plastic outer ring and a metal inner ring. This enables you to move the hoop quickly without taking the embroidery out of the machine as your stitching grows.

Painting and Dyeing Equipment
You will need a teaspoon, water spray, jug for mixing dye, and a cat litter tray or similarly sized and shaped vessel which will allow the silk cap to lay flat. A pair of tongs is useful for lifting out the wet silk cap. Inexpensive stiffly bristled brushes are ideal for working paint into silk caps and are also adequate for highlighting edges.

Wear a particle protection mask to prevent breathing in the fine dust of the dye powder, and work in a well ventilated space. Always adhere to the manufacturers safety directions. An apron and rubber gloves will help protect your skin and clothes.

Forming Equipment

For moulding the finished bowl you will need an appropriately sized pudding basin covered in cling film and a tubular object such as a tin on which to rest it, as the wet bowl needs to hang freely below the rim of the inverted basin. Make sure that the bowl is thoroughly dry before removing it from the basin.

All Projects Will Need:

Silk cap: Unless specified otherwise, a whole, undivided silk cap is used throughout

Cold water soluble film: 2 pieces each approx. 15"x15" (38 x 38cm), one placed beneath the silk cap and one on top, both secured in a

Spring loaded embroidery hoop: approx 9" (23cm) diameter

Stiffening spray: widely available, ready mixed

Cling film to help the bowl release from the mould

Pudding basin or other suitably sized and shaped mould

Tin or jar on which to stand the inverted basin

Sewing machine capable of free machining

Basic sewing kit

Dyeing and painting equipment (if not using a ready dyed cap or leaving the cap naturally coloured)

Choosing Materials

Silk Caps

All the bowls in this book are made out of mawata silk caps. The word 'mawata' comes from the Japanese and means 'to spread around'. Each cap is made from a cocoon which has been soaked in a special solution, then formed into shape over a mould. Once dried, the shape resembles a cap, hence the name. Its shape makes it ideal for creating embroidered bowls as it keeps its form. Caps can be bought dyed or undyed, but for the projects in this book I have dyed or painted each cap myself. With careful handling, each cap can be split into two or three layers, depending on the desired delicacy of the bowl you are making and the effect you are seeking. Once you have mastered the separating technique you should be able to produce at least two bowls from each cap.

Cold Water Soluble Film

There are many types of cold water soluble material on the market with new ones emerging all the time. For these bowls you need a film which is flexible and fine so that you can see where you are machining. I am currently using Solvy; this is a transluscent product which has a woven appearance, moves smoothly beneath the machine and washes out easily. For cutting out and applying shapes to the bowls I use Solusheet, which has the appearance of opaque disposable kitchen cloth. Solusheet is ideal for placing motifs as it is substantial enough to hold its shape once cut out.

Dyes and Paints

I use all-in-one acid dyes to colour the caps. These are quick and easy to use and need nothing added to the dye bath to assist the dyeing process. For some of the bowls I use silk paints to colour the caps instead. I often add a hint of metallic acrylic paint to the rims of the bowls to highlight the edges. These paints are available in a variety of colours from art and craft stores.

Threads

Threads made specifically for machine embroidery are finer than those made for normal machine stitching, as they do not have the tight twist or chemical treatment which mercerised thread needs in order to make it strong enough for sewing seams. Rayon machine embroidery threads come in many plain and variegated shades and give a lovely sheen to your work. Metallic threads come in a variety of forms. As well as plain gold, silver and copper there are coloured metallics, variegated metallics and those twisted with black. There are also unusual threads such as holographic ones, which tend to work better when used on the spool, to reduce the chances of the shredding to which they are prone. All threads should be stored in an airtight container away from direct sunlight to prevent them drying out and becoming brittle.

Fusible Polyester Fibres

These are loose fibres which once ironed flat, fuse together to form a sheet which will add a magical irridescence to your work. They may also be added as loose fibres. These products come in a variety of shades which can be mixed together for added interest. Take care not to over iron them as they melt and discolour very easily. I have used sheets of these fibres to line some of my bowls. The fibres are currently sold in the UK under a variety of brand names such as 'Angel Fibre', 'Angelina', and 'Crystalina'.

Beads and Sequins

Embellishing a finished bowl with seed beads and sequins hand stitched in place adds a different dimension to the piece. I use both glass and metallic beads , and both facetted and flat sequins on my bowls.

Fabric Stiffening Spray

This is a proprietary chemical product which allows fabric to be stiffened without altering its appearance or feel. A non toxic and non flammable spray, it can be sprayed onto the bowls to add stiffening without adversely affecting their quality as it does not react with any water soluble fabric still left in the silk. The spray is quick drying and if at first does not give the required stiffness, can be reapplied.
The spray can also be used at a later date to pep up a bowl which may have lost some of its original shape.

Safety Note

Although fabric stiffening sprays are generally non toxic, as when using any chemical, it is advisable to work in a well ventilated room and avoid breathing in the product.

Adding Colour

DYEING

Have a plentiful supply of hot water to hand. Keep the powdered dyes well away from the silk until you are ready to start the dyeing process. Just a tiny speck of dye powder on damp fabric goes a long way !

YOU WILL NEED:

A flat dye bath such as a cat litter tray or similar flat bottomed vessel
Jug for mixing the dyes
Teaspoons: a different one for each dye colour
Tongs for removing cap from dye bath
Rubber gloves
Fine particle face mask
Apron
Plastic to protect your work surface

ACID DYES

Silk and animal fibres such as wool, angora and mohair are made up of proteins and need acid in the dye bath to help assist the chemical bond between fibre and dye.
I use all-in-one acid dyes. These are quick and easy to use and need nothing added to the dye bath to assist the dyeing process.

SPACE DYEING

Thoroughly wet the silk cap in hot water and squeeze out the excess water.
Stretch out the cap and and lay it in the tray.
Lightly sprinkle the dye powders over the surface of the cap in the desired combination of colours, leaving space around the powders so that they can spread and blend.
TIP: You can dye more than one cap at a time by layering one on top of another. Add more powder to the top of the lower cap, letting the underside of the upper cap pick up dye from the one beneath.
At this stage I often add a little more hot water, just enough to keep the silk damp and blend the dye powders.
After 15 minutes, turn the cap or pile of caps over, and leave for a further 15 minutes.
Remove the caps from the dye bath and rinse thoroughly with tepid water until it runs clear.

Leave the caps to dry before using.
TIP: When making up a dye bath I always throw in any undyed threads I might need for hand stitching the bowl later, so that I have perfectly matching shades.

DIP DYEING

Thoroughly wet the silk cap and squeeze out the excess water.
Stretch out the cap and lay it in the dye bath.
Make up some dye in a jug by mixing one 5ml teaspoon to half a pint of boiling water.
Pour the dye mix over the silk cap and let it soak in.
Add more water if necessary. This amount is enough to dye several caps. Adjust the quantity of dye powder to the depth of colour you require.
Leave for half an hour before removing the caps and rinsing them thoroughly in tepid water.
Allow the caps to dry before using.
TIP: Exciting effects can be achieved by selectively dyeing separate areas of the cap.
(see Serengeti Bowl p36).

PAINTING

Painting can be used as an alternative to dyeing.
Fabric paints used for silk painting have to be heat fixed by ironing or steam fixing.
I have used iron fixable paints for the Four Seasons bowls (p26).

YOU WILL NEED:

A selection of fabric paints suitable for painting on silk, a stiff bristled paint brush, a sheet of polythene to protect the work surface.
Soak the silk cap thoroughly.
Dab off any excess water.
Stretch out the silk cap on the polythene.
Starting from the outer edge, paint the cap, moving towards the middle and adding different colours as required. Work quickly, brushing the paint into the cap. The colours will 'bleed' into each other and blend nicely.
Use the paints undiluted and spread them as if painting with water colours.
Leave the cap to dry. Once dry, you can set the paints by ironing.

Space Dyeing

Lay the silk cap in a non-food use tray and thoroughly dampen the cap with hot water.

Using non-food utensils, and wearing protective clothing, lightly sprinkle dry powder dye onto the wetted cap.

Add other colours to suit the design, leaving space between colours and varying the intensity of colour by lighter or heavier application of powder.

Gently pour small amounts of hot water over the colours, encouraging them to bleed into each other and also the spaces inbetween.

Agitate the colours, then following the dye manufacturer's instructions, leave to set (usually around 20 mins). Wash out the excess dye under running water. Leave the cap to dry.

Basic Bowl Technique

Organic shapes are a great starting point for embroidered bowls as the motifs can be worked spontaneously with no need for planned placement. Just as in nature, there cannot really be any 'mistakes', only natural variations.

Here, peacock feathers inspired a bowl of vivid greens and blues, embroidered in sparkling metallic threads. Heat fused polyester fibre adds a hint of glamour and sparkling organza makes the peacock 'eyes' gleam.

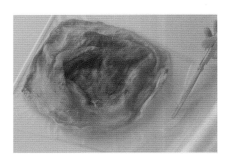

Dye a silk cap in your preferred shades and allow to dry thoroughly. Separate the silk cap into layers by peeling away gently at the outer edge. Most silk caps can be peeled into two or three layers. Place the silk cap on a piece of cold water soluble fabric slightly larger than the silk cap. If your water soluble fabric is not quite large enough, add small pieces to the bowl's outer edge later, as you stitch.

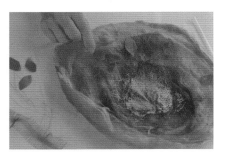

Place additional elements on top of the silk cap. Here, leaf shapes cut from synthetic organza form the peacock 'eyes'. Strands taken from the frayed edge of the same organza are sprinkled on to add glitter and texture. A piece of pre-ironed polyester fibre makes a beautiful focal point for the centre of the bowl.

Cut another piece of cold water soluble fabric to size as before. Place this over the silk cap and embellishments, forming a sandwich. Place the layered silk cap centrally in a spring clip hoop, gently easing until the cap lies smoothly and firmly within the hoop.

Set the sewing machine up for free machine embroidery(see Getting Started p6). Starting at the centre of the cap, bring the bobbin thread up through the fabric. Pull the bobbin and top threads out towards the rear of the machine and hold in place as you begin to stitch a spiral shape, working from the centre of the cap outwards.

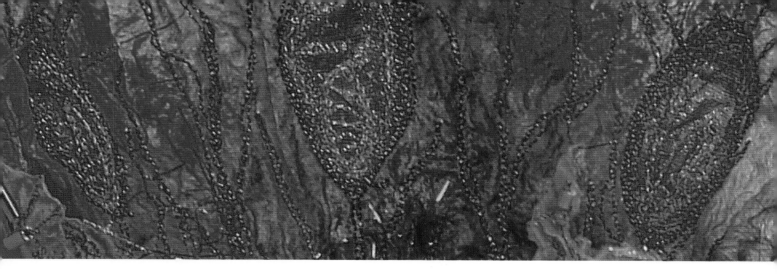

Continue to stitch outwards in a spiral until you have covered a sufficient area for what will become the base of your bowl. As a rough guide, the stitching shown here covers an area of approximately 4"(10cm).

Reposition the hoop and stitch radiating out from the centre of the spiral, towards the outer edge of the cap. Encapsulate the organza leaves within oval spirals of stitch worked over and around each shape. Continue stitching all around what will become the sides of the bowl in this way, repositioning the hoop as necessary. Stitch up to the edge of the silk cap, snipping into the cap's edge to flatten out the cap where necessary.

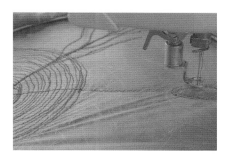

When machine stitching is complete, rinse the bowl briefly in cold water to remove almost all the water soluble film. Leaving a very tiny amount of film in the silk will help the finished bowl retain its shape.

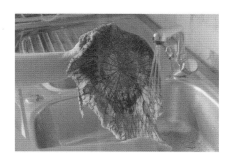

Place the bowl on a suitably shaped former, such as a pudding basin, which you have covered in cling film. The former needs to stand clear of the work surface so that the edges of the bowl can hang freely. Roughly tweak the bowl into your desired shape, fixing the folds in place by drying with a hairdryer if desired. When dry, spray with stiffening product and leave to dry again. Embellish the bowl with handstitching and beading.

Venetian

Inspired by a visit to Venice and John Ruskin's book 'The Stones of Venice', I designed the motif on this vivid bowl. On a subsequent visit to this beautiful city, I was delighted to see the actual cornice in St Mark's from which my design had originated.

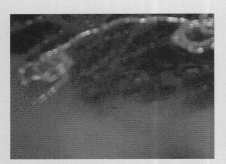

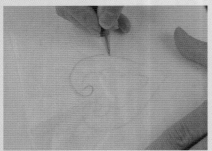

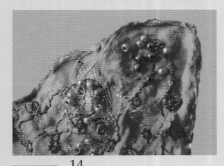

INGREDIENTS
Dye: Purple and pink
Threads: Purple, red and gold metallic
Fabric scraps: Gold metallic
Acrylic paint: Gold
Beads: Gold and pink metallic seed
Sequins: Facetted clear
Solusheet water soluble fabric: Approx. 3" x 24" (7.5cm x 61cm)

My Venetian bowls were the first designs I made using a more formal design than the usual flowing organic shapes which I so enjoy stitching. I knew that I would have to plan the placement of the motifs carefully to make the design work. Cutting out the shapes in Solusheet proved a simple way of ensuring perfect spacing before stitching.

Transferring and Applying Motifs

1 Trace the motif as many times as required onto Solusheet. Cut out each motif, leaving a 5mm gap around the edge of each one.

2 Position the motifs on top of the dyed silk cap. Scatter gold fabric scraps over the cap. Sandwich and frame the cap as usual (see basic techniques p10). Machine over the drawn outline of each motif with purple metallic thread before filling in with gold vermicelli stitch. Highlight the design with red thread.

3 Rinse and mould the bowl. Once dry, embellish with beads and sequins. Paint the edge of the bowl inside and out with gold acrylic paint.

See a glowing orange version of this design on p4

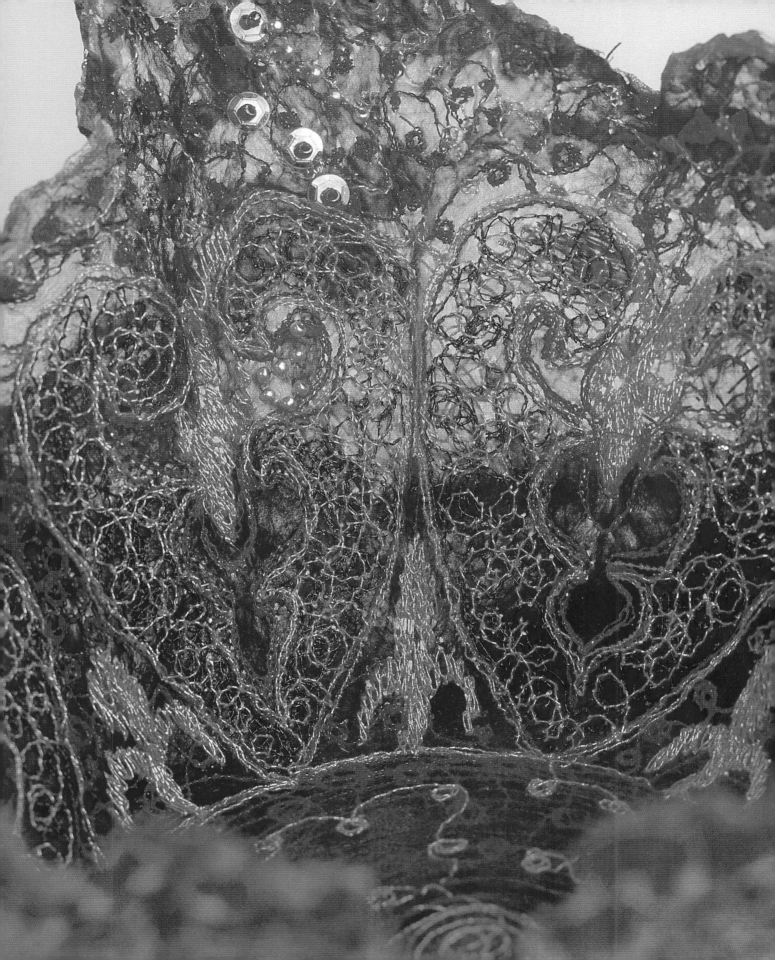

Oceanic

On a trip to the Great Barrier Reef I went in a semi submersible (never again !) and was fascinated to find that the ocean looked nothing like the brightly coloured photographs I'd seen; which are taken using specialist lighting. My bowl shows the contrast between the real and artificially enhanced views of the ocean's beautiful shades.

INGREDIENTS
Dye: Marine blue and malachite
Threads: Blue and green metallic, orange and red rayon
Fabric scraps: Metallic or glitzy organza
Beads: Blue and gold assorted
Sequins: Blue and gold, 1/8" (3mm) flat bluey green for the fish eyes
Fusible polyester fibre: Blue shades, applied as a sheet
Solusheet water soluble fabric approx 3" x 24" (7.5cm x 61cm)

Although some of the bowls in this book are of subdued, natural tones, this design gives full rein to the more colourful side of my creativity. The ocean is a wonderfully rich design source and can be interpreted in many ways from the restrained to the fantastic. Experiment with colour combinations you might not normally try, and prepare to be surprised (and delighted !) at the results.

Double Sided Designs

1 Prepare the cap as usual, placing a sheet of heat fixed polyester fibre in the centre of the cap. Cut fish shapes from metallic fabric. You will need two of each shape, placed one on either side of the cap so they align.
2 Sandwich and frame the cap in the usual way. Machine each fish in place with several rows of stitching around its edge and across it in a diamond design.
3 Stitch fins and a tail around the fish. With metallic thread on top and red or orange on the bobbin, machine the rest of the cap with vermicelli stitch before sewing the coral in place around the fish.
Rinse, mould and dry the bowl.
4 Decorate with beads and sequins.

Malachite and indigo shades recreate the ocean's depths

Bridal

These delicate bowls, based on the honeysuckle motif I used on my daughter Sarah's wedding dress, make charming mementoes of a special day. The smaller bowl can be used as a favour dish or ring container, in place of the more usual cushion.

INGREDIENTS

Threads: Silver metallic, holographic, plus rayon threads in pale pink and green, also variegated peach/cream
Beads: pearls, silver bugle, small crystal
Sequins: Mother of pearl effect
Fusible polyester fibre: White holographic, applied as a sheet

Prepare a divided silk cap as usual, adding a sheet of heat fixed fibre (see below) in the centre of the cap before adding the top layer of water soluble film.
Cover the cap with vermicelli stitch, using silver thread on the top and holographic thread on the bobbin.
Embroider the stems and leaves of the honeysuckle in pale green thread. With variegated thread on the top and pale pink thread on the bobbin, embroider the honeysuckle flowers.
Having rinsed, formed and dried the bowl in the usual way, hand embellish with beads and sequins. The smaller bowl is made with the second layer peeled from the silk cap.

Adding Sparkle and Sheen

1 Place some shredded fusible fibre on a sheet of baking parchment. Snip the fibres as necessary if some of them are too long to arrange into a piece of the desired size.
2 Place a second piece of baking parchment on top of the shredded fibres. Press briefly but firmly with an iron set to a medium setting. If the iron is too hot, the fibres will discolour. If the iron is too cold, the fibres will not fuse, so some experimentation may be needed to achieve the desired effect.

A glittering dragonfly adds magic. (see p38/40)

Lizard

I have been fascinated by lizards since childhood, when they were abundant in our garden. I remember grabbing a lizard and being horrified as it wriggled away leaving me holding its tail. I was inconsolable until my father explained that this was how a lizard escaped from a predator, and a replacement tail would soon grow.

INGREDIENTS

Dye: Forest green
Threads: Greens and brown rayons, variegated Natesh, holographic
Fabric scraps: Gold metallic
Acrylic paint: Gold
Beads: Assorted green seed and bugle, gold seed for centres of lizards' eyes
Sequins: Black, for lizards' eyes
Fusible polyester fibre: 'Forest Blaze', applied as a sheet
Solusheet water soluble fabric: approx 8" x 24" (20cm x 61cm)

Trace the lizard template onto Solusheet. Cut out five lizard shapes. Place one layer of a silk cap on top of the water soluble film. Add the fusible polyester fibre and lizard motifs before covering with a second layer of water soluble film. Secure all layers in an inverted embroidery hoop.
Using a dark green thread, start machining from the centre of the bowl, working outwards in a circular motion to form the base. Stitch the ferns. Using the variegated threads, machine the lizards in satin stitch, covering the Solusheet forms completely. Finish machining the ferns.

Beyond the Edge; Stitching in Thin Air

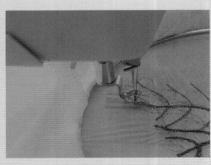

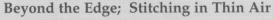

1 Using light green thread on the top and holographic thread on the bobbin, lay down an undulating mesh of stitch to extend the fern beyond the cap's edge.
2 Using dark green thread top and bottom, lay down the main stems of the fern in straight stitch, over the mesh.
3 Work satin stitch over each branch of the fern.
Rinse and mould the bowl (see basic techniques p12). Once dry, paint the edge of the bowl inside and out with silver acrylic paint.

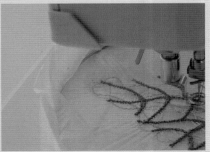

To make a lizard, machine satin stitch over a wire armature mounted in a hoop on cold water soluble film. Add bugle and seed beads.

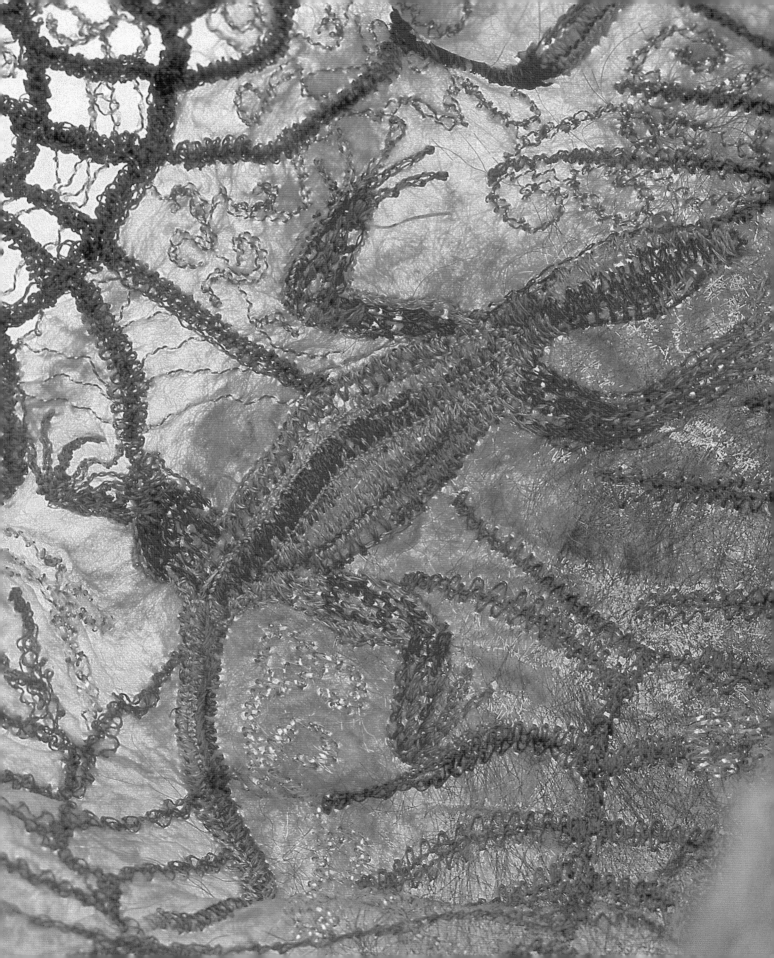

Chinese Dragon

My eldest daughter Sarah, an avid collector of all things dragon inspired requested that I make her a suitably themed bowl. This Chinese dragon guarding the treasure in his fiery lair was the incandescent result. While the bowl was drying, I pulled the edges until they resembled flames.

INGREDIENTS

Dye: Red and orange
Threads: Metallic gold and copper, rayon red, crimson and orange
Fabric scraps: Gold and copper metallic
Acrylic paint: Gold
Beads: Gold
Sequins: Facetted copper
Solusheet cold water soluble fabric: approx 8" x 24" (20cm x 61cm)

Prepare a cap. Scatter scraps of gold metallic fabric over the cap before securing as usual. Using the same coloured thread in the top and bottom of the machine, stitch a yin yang motif centrally on the cap; work one half in orange and the other in red. Working outwards from the centre, stitch flames in red and orange threads. Work the dragon in gold thread. Follow basic techniques p12 to finish. Highlight areas of flame and the outside of the dragon with gold acrylic paint. Affix sequins for the dragon's eyes and accentuate the flames with beads and sequins.

Machine Lace Bowl with Fabric Fragments

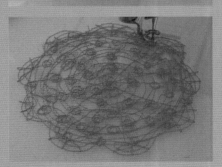

1 Trap some snippets of copper metallic fabric between two layers of cold water soluble film and secure in an inverted hoop. Using a toning rayon thread, straight stitch from the centre outwards in a spiral, ensuring that all fabric pieces are incorporated.
2 Stitch from the centre outwards in a daisy petal shape to form a grid.
3 Stitch small circles at the intersections of the grid. Highlight with gold thread.
4 Work a scalloped edge around the perimeter. Shape and dry.

This lacy bowl makes a pretty trinket holder

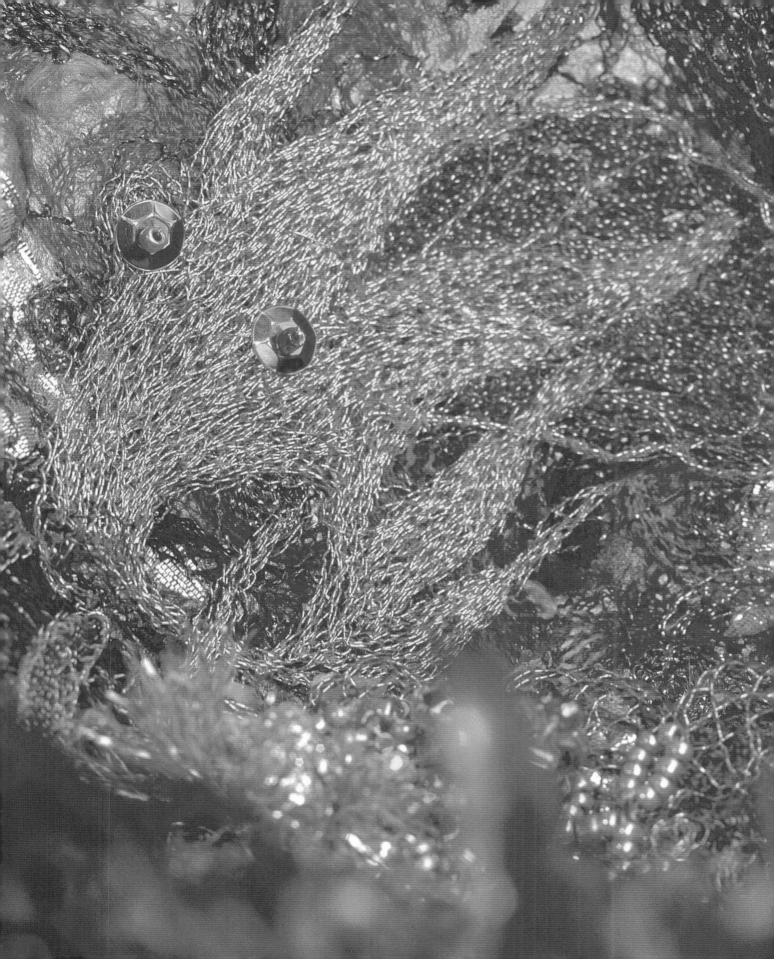

Riverside

On a riverside walk in Salisbury, England, I watched the dragonflies emerge from their casings, crawl up the reeds to dry off and then fly away. I was inspired to make the Riverside bowl. I wanted it to resemble Tiffany glass and have a dragonfly which looked as though it was still wet, basking in the sun.

INGREDIENTS
Dye: Green and yellow
Threads: Metallic greens and browns
Fabric scraps: Gold and green glitzy
Acrylic paint: Gold
Beads: A variety of toning seed
Sequins: Facetted copper

Place a space dyed silk cap on a piece of water soluble film. Place some leaf shapes cut from the gold and green fabrics on top of the silk cap beneath another layer of water soluble fabric. Secure all layers in an inverted embroidery hoop. Using green thread, machine freely all over the cap, making the embroidery as dense as you wish to represent the vegetation on a river bank. Rinse, mould and dry the bowl (see basic techniques p12) before embellishing (see below).

Needle Weaving and Beading

1 When the bowl is dry, thread a fine, sharp needle with metallic thread and begin to needleweave an impressionistic cobweb between two points around the bowl's rim.
2 Using a beading needle threaded with the same thread as for the cobweb, embellish the web and the bowl rim with a few beads.

Learn how to make a dragonfly on p38/40

Four Seasons

I was good at art at school but I could also be lazy. I dashed off some tree sketches for homework in about ten minutes. My teacher's comment was "Have you ever seen trees that look like this? Next time, draw them from life." These days I always carefully observe whatever I am sketching or stitching !

INGREDIENTS
Threads: Blue rayon, brown metallic and holographic
Acrylic paint: Silver
Beads: Crystal seed and silver bugle
Sequins: Facetted holographic and 3mm flat silver
Fusible polyester fibre: 'Cobalt Sparkle', applied as a sheet
Glitter Gel: 'Crystal Glitter'

1. Place the silk cap on a piece of water soluble film. Lay the prepared fusible polyester fibre in the centre and tear off some pieces to scatter around the rest of the cap. Continue the normal preparation for stitch.
2. With blue as the top thread and holographic thread on the bobbin, build up the base with circular stitching. Cover the whole cap with vermicelli stitch.
3. With brown metallic thread, stitch the tree trunks evenly around the centre of the bowl, starting from the perimeter of the base. Work the branches spreading outwards to meet around the bowl's edge. Stitch vegetation beneath the trees.
4. Once the stitching is complete and the bowl has been washed, shaped and dried, embellish with beads and sequins.
The other seasons' bowls can be made in the same way, varying the colours as shown on p28/29.

Silk paint effects

1 Thoroughly wet one layer of a silk cap. Pat off excess water. Place the cap in a flat bottomed vessel. Working quickly, using a fairly stiff brush apply blue silk paint all around the perimeter of the cap.
2 Add scant dashes of purple just inside the blue painted 'sky'. Rewet the silk cap with a water spray to encourage the colours to blend if necessary. Leave the middle of the cap unpainted to represent snow. The paint should soak right through the cap. If you need to turn it over and paint the other side, wipe the tray clean before you lay the cap back down. Leave the cap to dry.

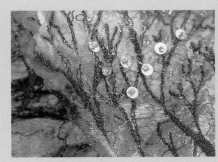

Holographic threads and fibres add a frosty feel

SPRING

ADDITIONAL INGREDIENTS
Black, lilac and green rayon threads
Lilac seed beads

1 Prepare the cap for stitching as usual. Scatter pieces of heat fixed polyester fibre around the outer edge of the cap in the 'sky' area before you start stitching.

2 Using green thread, start stitching in the centre of the cap, working in a circle as before. Work vermicelli stitch in blue and holographic threads all over the cap.

3 Once you have machined the tree trunks and branches, stitch green leaves in place. Work the vegetation beneath the trees in green. Use lilac thread to represent bluebells in the grass. Stitch birds in black. When the bowl has been rinsed, moulded and dried, add lilac seed beads at the foot of the trees.

Paint all the caps on these pages in the same way as the Winter design, but this time paint the centres green to represent vegetation.

SUMMER

ADDITIONAL INGREDIENTS
White stranded cotton
Gold seed beads

1 Paint the cap as for Spring.

2 Prepare and work as for Spring, but make the stitching for the leaves much denser to represent the trees in full leaf.

3 When the bowl has been rinsed, moulded and dried, stitch French knots in white thread among the green vegetation beneath the trees. Add gold seed beads to the upper branches.

AUTUMN

ADDITIONAL INGREDIENTS
Orange, red and brown thread
Brown paint
Copper and gold seed beads

1 Paint the centre of the cap brown. Stitch the base in brown thread to depict fallen leaves.

2 Prepare and stitch as before, but using oranges, browns and red threads for the leaves. Stitch the vegetation beneath the trees in brown.

3 When the bowl has been rinsed, moulded and dried, add copper and gold seed beads as desired.

Rainforest Quartet

This set of bowls was inspired by a vertigo inducing cable car ride high above the dense foliage of the Kurada rainforest, North West Australia. I wanted the main bowl to resemble an epiphyte; the type of air plant which was all around us, growing on the branches and the trunks of the trees.

Dye: Green and brown (plus orange for dyeing throwsters' waste)
Threads: Rayon threads in greens and browns
Fabric scraps: Copper coloured metallic effect
Acrylic paint: Gold Metallic
Beads: Gold
Sequins: Facetted copper
Scraps of left over pieces of silk cap for the two smaller bowls.
Orange silk fibres (De-gummed throwsters' waste dyed orange)

Sometimes I become so caught up in a theme that I make not just one or two, but as here, a whole quartet of bowls exploring a single idea. Each one develops from the last, and they look beautiful when displayed singly; stunning when shown as an ensemble.

Working a whole collection of bowls based around one theme is a great way to broaden your expertise and explore your creativity.

Here, I have used a diversity of techniques which all build from the same basic method. Wired petals, layering different colour caps and beading are all employed here to dramatic effect.

Playing With Texture

1 Dye the silk cap green. When dry, divide into two layers. Place one layer on the first piece of water soluble film. The second layer is used to make the smaller bowls. Cut some of the metallic fabric scraps into leaf shapes and arrange them on the cap. Place some throwsters' waste randomly around the cap. Prepare for stitching in the usual way. Machine from the centre outwards in a circular motion. Once you have built up a solid base, start working towards the edges of the bowl.

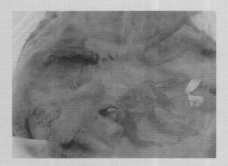

2 Machine around the edges and over the metallic fabric leaf shapes. Cut deeply into the edges of the bowl so that it resembles thick blades of grass. Machine along these to create an impression of veined leaves. When the stitching is complete, rinse and shape the bowl in the usual way. When dry, embellish with beads and sequins. Highlight the bowl's edge with gold paint.

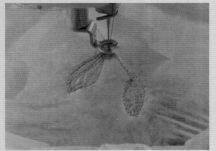

Make a glittering bug, see p40

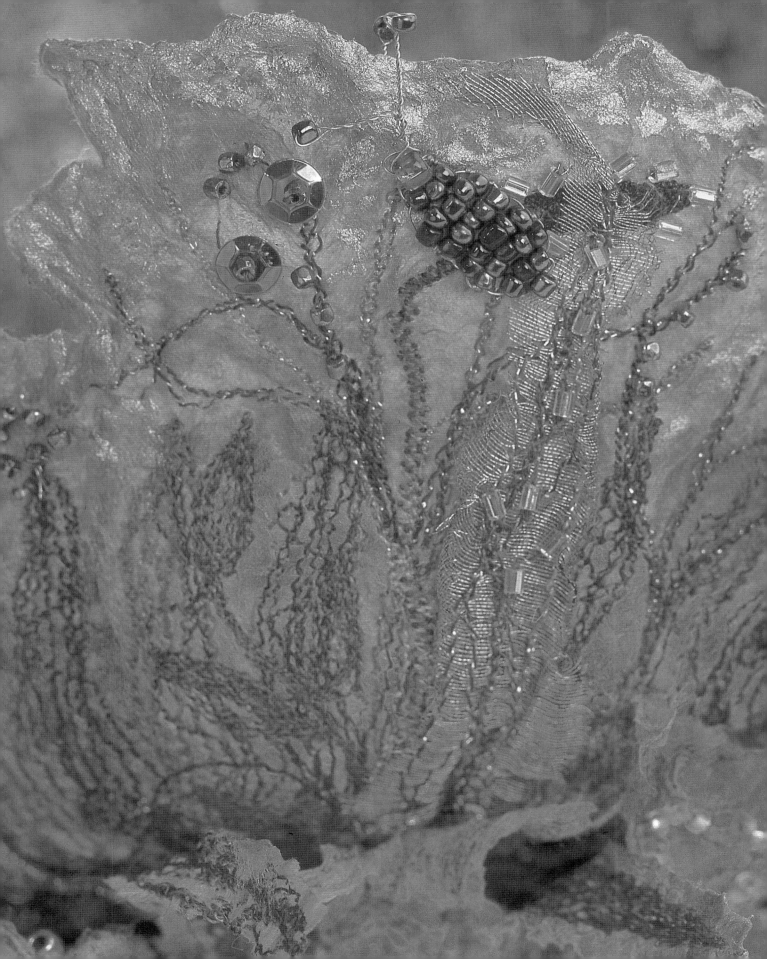

Rainforest Layered

The second Rainforest bowl shows the effect that can be achieved by layering separated caps dyed in different colours on top of each other before stitching.

To replicate this look, place a fine layer of green silk cap over a thicker layer of brown cap. Once machine stitched as desired, rinse away the water soluble film and mould the bowl as usual, leaving the two layers of silk cap fused together.

The small bugs are made from wire and beads. One is brightly coloured and the other plain gold to represent a male and female. Placing one bug on the inside and one bug directly opposite on the outside of the bowl gives the impression that they are crawling towards each other for a romantic assignation! This bowl also features a beaded bodied dragon fly. See p38/40 for details of how to make beaded and winged bugs.

Tiny Fronds

This tiny bowl has deeply cut petal shaped edges. Machine fine wire in place centrally along each petal so that you can curve the bowl like a waterlily.

1 Prepare a small piece of green silk cap for stitching in the usual way, incorporating five copper metallic fabric leaf shapes in the design. Stitch outwards from the centre in a circular pattern to create the bowl's base. Secure the leaves with stitching. Work vermicelli stitch across the entire surface.

2 Form the end of a length of wire into a circular shape, leaving the other end long enough to extend to the outer edge of the bowl. Secure by working zig zag stitch across the wire. Lay a second length of wire in a U shape with the base of the U abutting the central wire circle. Zig zag in place. Repeat with a third length of wire.

3 Add green metallic organza leaves inbetween the copper leaves and secure in place with stitch. Stitch a wavy edge around the bowl's perimeter. Rinse and mould the bowl as shown in basic techniques and leave to dry. When dry, embellish with beads as desired.

Wired Flower

This bowl features a metallic flower motif and sequins.

Egyptian

The 50th birthday of my friend Valerie merited a very special gift. She had just visited Egypt so I made her a bowl featuring the Egyptian symbols of the Ankh for life, the Lotus for birth and dawn, and the Scarab; the little dung rolling beetle, a symbol of regeneration and spontaneous creation.

INGREDIENTS
Dye: Blue and turquoise
Threads: Blue, green and red, plus gold metallic
Fabric scraps: Blue and green glitzy metallic look
Acrylic paint: Gold
Beads: Gold
Sequins: Facetted blue

Place a silk cap onto a piece of cold water soluble film. Trace the lotus design onto tracing paper (see template at back of book) and cut out. Cut the lotus base and large petals from blue metallic fabric and the medium sized petals from green metallic fabric. You will need four lotus motifs. To position these accurately, fold the cap into quarters and mark with pins before placing the motifs. Trap these in place between the cap and a top layer of water soluble film. Secure all layers in an inverted embroidery hoop. Using matching threads, machine embroider backwards and forwards over the metallic pieces, making sure you embroider right up to their edges. Embroider the upper petals using red thread. Fill the gaps between the motifs with embroidered gold crosses.

Adding Painted Highlights

When you have rinsed and moulded the bowl (see basic techniques), paint the edges with gold acrylic paint inside and out. Embellish with the sequins and gold beads.

The ancient Egyptians believed that the sun was rolled across the sky by a dung beetle. *To make him, see p42*

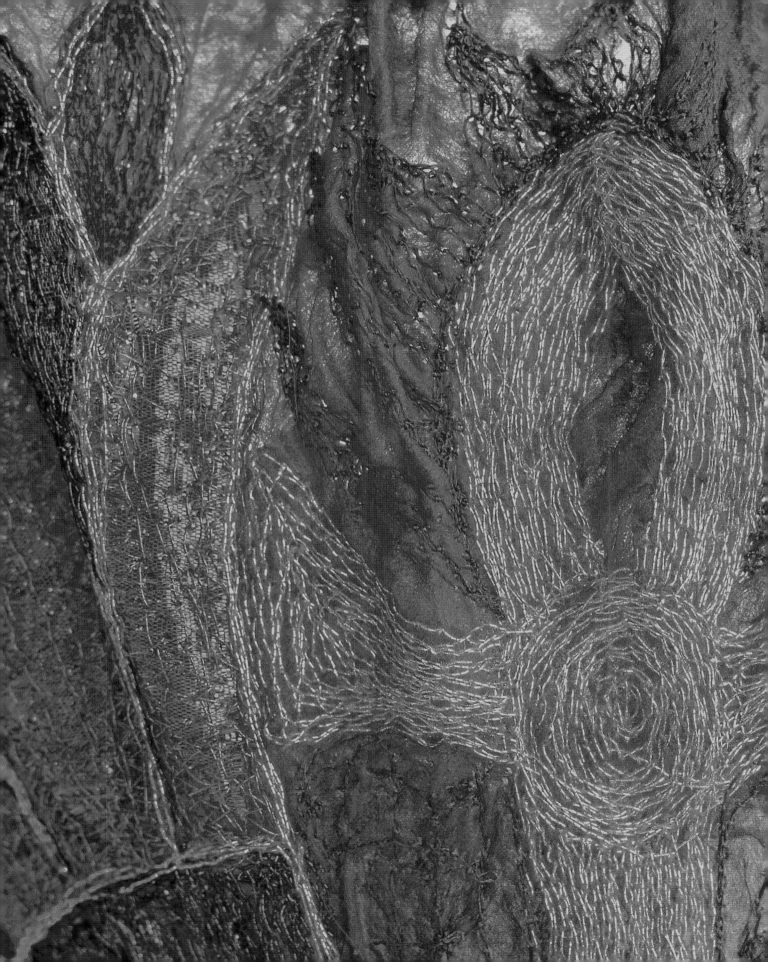

Serengeti

Asked to produce an intensely coloured bowl, I was inspired by a lovely photograph in a travel magazine, which showed an acacia tree silhouetted against a brilliant sunset. For some time I had been toying with the idea of depicting animals and decided to incorporate them here in silhouette form.

INGREDIENTS
Dye: Yellow, orange and brown
Threads: Black, yellow and orange rayon
Solusheet water soluble fabric: 1 piece approx 6" x 24" (15cm x 61cm)

Place the larger cap on top of a piece of water soluble film, adding a second piece of film on top. Secure all the layers in an inverted embroidery hoop. Starting from the centre, cover the whole piece with vermicelli stitch, matching the threads to the dye colours as you stitch. Machine the trees in satin stitch and straight stitch. Trace the giraffe template four times onto the Solusheet and cut them out leaving 5mm around the edge. Position the giraffes, anchoring them beneath a piece of film large enough to fit the hoop. With the stitch width set to the widest satin stitch position, stitch the giraffes and tree trunks in black thread. Rinse out and mould the bowl (see basic techniques p12).

Dip Dyeing

1 Following the dye manufacturer's directions, dye a silk cap yellow.

2 Make up a small amount of brown dye and dip the middle of the cap into it.

3 Make up a small quantity of orange dye and dip the outer edge of the cap into it.

4 When dry, separate the cap in two. Set the smaller cap aside.

Big cats prowl around the base of an alternative design, made from the smaller silk cap section.

Winged Creatures

Winged creatures such as this pretty dragonfly are amazingly quick and easy to make. The bodies use the simple beading technique shown on p40/41. Stitching the wings is the work of moments. These creatures are an enchanting addition to any bowl. Add a brooch fitting so that the creature can be detached for use as a decorative accessory.

For the Wings
INGREDIENTS
Shot effect organza approx 5" x 12" (13cm x 30.5cm)
Cold Water soluble film: 2 pieces each approx 13" x 13' (33cm x 33cm)
Variegated pastel metallic machine embroidery thread
Soldering Iron

For the Body
INGREDIENTS AND METHOD:
See page 40/41

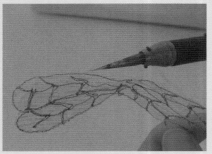

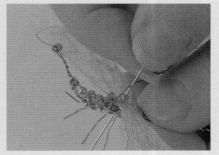

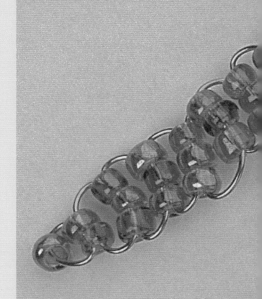

1 Place the organza on one piece of water soluble film. Add the second piece of water soluble film and secure all layers in an inverted embroidery hoop. With your machine set up for free stitchery, using metallic thread both on the top and in the spool, carefully stitch the outline of the wings in straight stitch. Machine the veins of the wings, making sure that these stitches connect with the stitched outline so that the wings will be strong.

2 Cut away the excess organza, rinse away the water soluble film and leave the wings to dry.
When the wings are dry, snip away any excess fabric from around the perimeter stitch line. Clean up and seal these delicate edges by lightly touching them with a soldering iron, preferrably fine tipped.

3 Stitch the wings to the back of the dragonfly's body. Cover the stitching with a few extra beads if desired.

Beaded Bugs

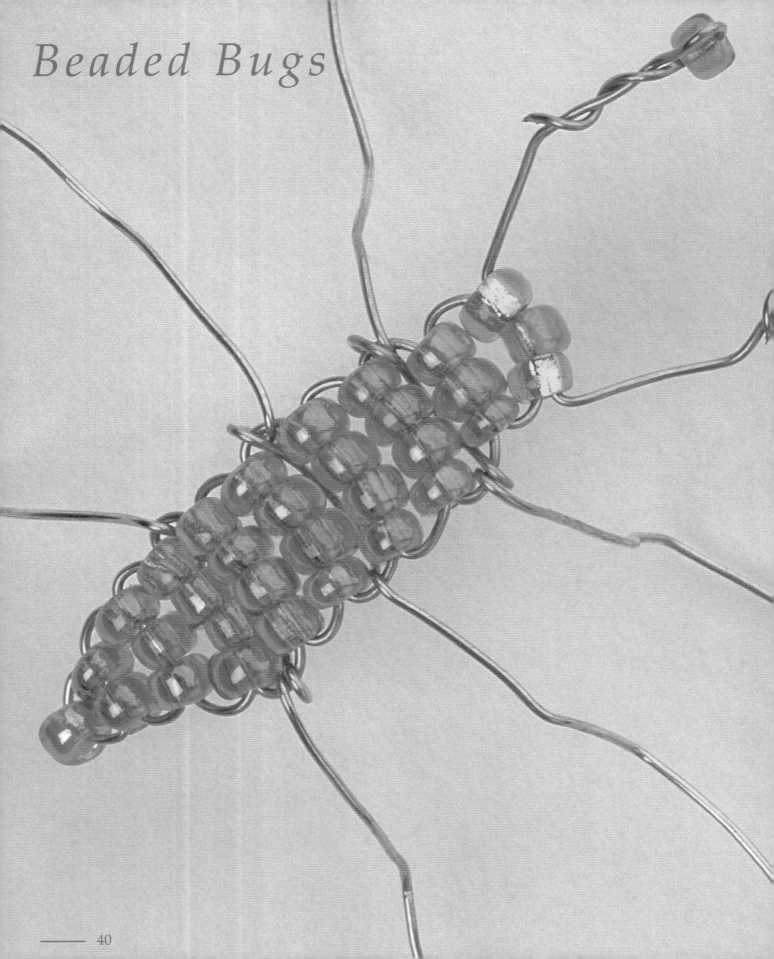

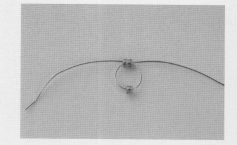

The glittering complexity of these beaded bugs belies the simplicity of the technique by which they are created. Threading, looping and tightening off each row of beads is surprisingly soothing and you will quickly see the potential for producing all sorts of beaded beauties of your own.

The **dragonfly** on p38/39 is made in exactly the same way as the basic bug shown here; but with 19 rows of beads worked at step 3 and an initial wire length of 30" (76cm). A pair of round nosed pliers and a set of small wire snips, although not essential, make light work of bending and cutting the wire; and mean that your best scissors will live to see another day! Kitchen or floristry scissors are a good alternative to wire cutters if you can't wait to have a go.

INGREDIENTS
Beading wire
Small round glass beads in green and gold

1 Fold a 12" (30cm) piece of wire in half to mark the middle. Thread three beads onto the wire. Hold one bead at the centre of the wire. Take a loose end of the wire and pass it through the middle of the other two beads, forming a loop. Pull the wire tight.

2 Thread three beads onto one wire and pass the other wire back through these. Pull the wire tight.

3 Thread four beads onto one wire and pass the other wire back through these. Pull the wire tight. Repeat this step for three more rows.

4 Add a row of three beads.

5 Add a row of three beads; one gold, one green, one gold, securing as before. Add a single bead for the tip of each antenna. Bend the wire around this bead and twist two or three times around the antenna before trimming off the excess.

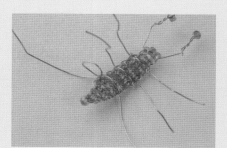

To Make the Legs:
Cut three lengths of wire each 2 1/2" (6cm) long. Pick up one length. Loop the end of this wire through and around the wire at the side of the bug's body below the head. Take the wire beneath the body. Repeat the process at the other side. Repeat for the other two legs spacing them evenly.

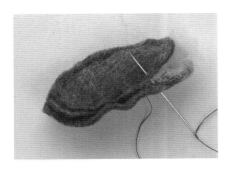

Ingredients:
Mounting board: One body piece from template
Black felt: Four body pieces, one pincer piece
Black organza: One body piece + 2cm seam allowance
Shot metallic 'beetle' coloured fabric: One body piece + 2cm seam allowance
Small piece of polyester wadding
Two black sequins
Black polyester thread
Black stranded embroidery thread
27" (68.5cm) 26 gauge brass craft wire
Double sided sticky tape
Tracing paper (see p44 for body and pincers templates)

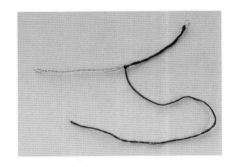

Method:
Trim down two of the felt body pieces so that each is slightly smaller than the last. Set one large felt body piece aside.
Stack the other three felt body pieces on top of each other with the smallest piece on the top.
Using black polyester thread and small running stitches, stitch all the pieces together. Insert a small amount of wadding between the smallest body piece and its neighbour before closing with the stitching.
Put a strip of double sided tape onto the card and stick the body, smallest felt piece down, onto it.
Place the organza on top of the metallic fabric.
Using a doubled length of polyester thread, sew a row of tiny running stitches all around the perimeter approximately 1/2" (1.5cm) away from the edge.
Place the layered fabric over the felted body, organza side facing up.
Pull the gathering stitches tight so that the fabric fits snugly over the domed body. Trim away any excess fabric.
Fasten off the gathering stitches on the underside of the body and lace securely across the card with additional stitches.

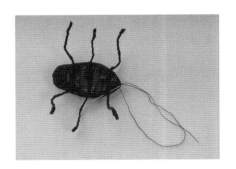

For the legs:
Cut three pieces of wire each approximately 9" (23cm) long.
Fold each piece of wire in half, bringing the ends towards the middle and twist together, working from the ends towards the centre. Flatten the looped ends slightly to form the beetle's feet.
Using three strands of stranded embroidery thread, wrap the wire entirely except for the small loops. Repeat with two more pieces of wire.
Place the pincer piece of felt at the head of the body and stitch to the underside of the body fabric.
Stitch the legs in place on the underside of the body. Cover the beetle's underbelly with the last piece of felt. Oversew neatly all round.
Sew two sequins on the head for eyes. Mark the division between the head, body and wings with simple hand stitches.

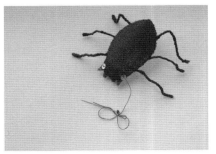

Beetle

This padded fabric beetle
borrows the stumpwork
technique of layering graded
pieces of felt to produce a
domed effect. It is easy to
see how you can adapt the
technique to produce a whole
range of bugs and beasties.

Motifs & Templates

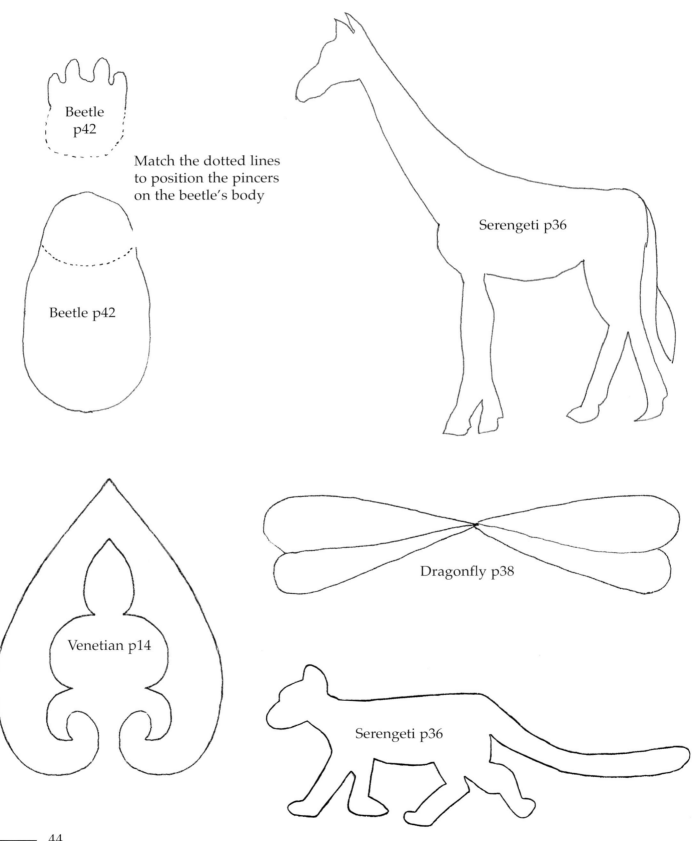

Beetle
p42

Match the dotted lines
to position the pincers
on the beetle's body

Beetle p42

Serengeti p36

Venetian p14

Dragonfly p38

Serengeti p36

Dragon p22

Use the head and tail
templates and adjust
the length of the body
to suit the size of your
bowl

Glossary

Armature
A supporting framework, usually constructed of wire, for a 3D piece.

Cold Water Soluble Film
A non-woven fabric which will wash away when immersed in cold water.

Dip Dyeing
A controlled dyeing method in which the cap is selectively dipped into a dye solution.

Feed Dogs/Teeth
The serrated teeth beneath the machine bed which 'feed' the fabric along. These need to be lowered or covered when free machining, so that the fabric is free for the embroiderer to manipulate as desired.

Fusible Polyester Fibres; also known by brand names such as '**Angel Fibre**', '**Angelina**' or '**Crystalina**'.
A glittery, light reflective polyester fibre available in a host of colours. This versatile and exciting fibre can be ironed between two sheets of non-stick baking parchment to make a smooth fabric for adding to projects. Alternatively, scatter loose strands onto the silk cap and incorporate with stitch for a very different effect.

Silk Cap
A silk cocoon which has been wetted, then stretched over a bowl and left to dry. The unspun silk forms a cap shape which may be separated into layers for delicate effects.

'Solusheet' (brand name) Cold Water Soluble Fabric
A cold water soluble fabric perfect for applying and placing motifs.

Space Dyeing
A random dyeing method in which the fabric is wetted thoroughly before dye powder is sprinkled onto the wet surface and allowed to spread and blend.

Spring Loaded Embroidery Hoop
An embroidery frame with a plastic outer hoop and a metal inner hoop. Squeezing the handles on the metal hoop together, this hoop is placed inside the plastic hoop, before releasing the handles to secure the fabric between the two. This type of hoop can be easily repositioned while the work is still in the sewing machine, making it a perfect choice for this type of stitching.

Health and Safety

Remember that dyes are chemicals and should be handled with care.
Always dye in a well ventilated room, away from food preparation areas.
Powdered acid dyes are very fine so care should be taken when handling them.
Avoid eye contact If dye splashes into the eye, irrigate immediately with clean water or eye wash solution for at least 15 minutes. Seek medical advice if a problem arises.
Ingestion Rinse mouth and drink plenty of water. Do not induce vomiting. Seek medical advice.
Inhalation Dye powders are known to be irritants to the respiratory system.
If symptoms similar to hay fever or asthma develop, seek medical advice.
People known to be suffering from asthma or chronic chest disease should avoid handling these dyes.
Keep dyes stored in clearly marked containers in a dry place, out of reach of pets and children.
Keep all the equipment use for dyeing well away from that used for food preparation.

Acknowledgements

I would like to acknowledge the following people, without whose support this book would not have been produced.

Thankyou to my family; my husband Geoff and my children: Sarah, Brian and Clare who have lived with a 'student' mum for the last few years and have been unable to eat in the dining room because of all my work being on the table.

Thanks to my tutor Christine Cook who 'made' me make the first bowl.

I would like to thank my friends: Val, Kate and Pam who gave me the push to get publishing.

I would also like to thank Val for the loan of the Egyptian Bowl. Thank you to my two fellow students Janet and Jennifer for helping to keep my sanity with our HNC playdays.

Lastly, I would like to thank the two wonderful people who made this whole book possible; Deena Beverley and Andrew Newton-Cox. Their encouragement and enthusiasm for this project has been an inspiration to me.

Kath Danswan, Wiltshire, England

Index of Techniques

Kath Danswan was taught to embroider from an early age by her mother and grandmother, and developed her love of nature with her father.

Following her City and Guilds Embroidery Parts One and Two, Kath's final collection for her HNC in Stitched Textiles featured the machine embroidered bowls for which she has since become renowned.

She now teaches machine embroidery and felt-making, and gives talks and workshops around the globe. Kath also exhibits widely and accepts commissions.

An enthusiastic member of the Embroiderers' Guild, Kath has written for its magazine, 'Embroidery', as well as for the specialist textile website, 'Workshop on the Web'.

When she is not stitching, Kath sings with her local Choral Society and Gilbert and Sullivan Society. Her needlecraft skills are often called into play when the producer wants unusual props. A shoal of startlingly realistic larger than life fish, complete with detachable skeletons, was a highlight of a recent production of 'Ruddigore'.

Kath lives in Wiltshire, England. She and husband Geoff have three children.

www.danswandesigns.co.uk

Suppliers

Threads, silk fabric paints and fabric stiffening spray are widely available from art and craft stockists.
The following specialist suppliers have kindly supplied tools and materials:

Soldering irons (fine tipped)
Margaret Beal
01264 365102
burningissues@margaretbeal.co.uk

Sewing Machines
Bernina
www.bernina.co.uk

Silk Caps (space dyed)
Kath Danswan
01793 533268
www.danswandesigns.co.uk

Scissors
Fiskars
www.fiskars.com

Solvy cold water soluble film (for all bowls)
Solusheet cold water soluble fabric
(for motifs)
Husqvarna Studio
0115 9881552
www.husqvarnastudio.co.uk

Iron
Morphy Richards
www.morphyrichards.co.uk

Dyes
Omega Dyes
01453 823691
www.omegadyes.co.uk

Silk Caps (undyed)
Rainbow Silks
01494 862111
www.rainbowsilks.co.uk

Beads, Angel Fibre, Beading Wire,
Pliers and Wire Cutters
Whichcraft
01142 661714
www.whichcraft.info

Tiny Sequins
Janice Williams
01452 740639

Overseas Stockists:

Fantasy Fibre
Art Institute Glitter Inc.
www.artglitter.com

Stiffen Stuff
Beacon Adhesives
www.beaconadhesives.com

Cold Water Soluble Film
Sulky of America,
www.sulky.com